On *Love*

Z I S H A   S

COVER DESIC
ART BY REYALDO LOGRO...

Cover Design by Maria L Evans
Art by Reyaldo Logrono

PAGE PUBLISHING, INC.
Conneaut Lake, PA

First originally published by Page Publishing 2020

ISBN 978-1-64544-748-1 (pbk)
ISBN 978-1-64544-749-8 (digital)

Printed in the United States of America

CONTENTS

MOM'S BOY

Boy hug his mom very tight.
His dad was not in sight
A radiant joy, little boy was
like living in heaven above.

Mom and boy would walk through the park.
Singing old songs straight from the heart.
Times were great, no dad around.
Sweet, loving mom made boy so proud.

Private school was just fun.
Friends, sports, and pretty girls too
Mom's boy had plenty things to do.

Mom's boy made his way on the stage.
With diploma, shook hands and waved.
Mom was proud, couldn't hold her tears
For a high school graduate on parade,
completion of resolution she made.

College was not so bad.
Mom's boy was the head of his class.
As he studied hard to make Mom glad.

To restrain Mom from extreme bliss
Hugged mom and showed her his degree
Put it close so her eyes would see.

Jobs were waiting for boy to claim.
He accepted one and made a name.

Mom's boy was very big now.
His sweetheart was ready for that vow.
No dad interest in boy's life yet.
Nevertheless, boy had no regrets.
When the couple repeated "I do,"
Boy kissed both, bride and Mom too.

It was not easy when Mom passed.
Pain and grief last and last.
The couple grew closer together.
Shared their love with two kids they had.
Care for your family, all you can.
Mom taught boy to be a family man.

Unexpected, Mom's boy passed away.
With grief and pain that sickness brings.

The cycle returned, Mom and two.
To carry on and make it through.
A good life, though short, she said they had.

Oh! God!
What made you mad!

2011

MOM'S BOY

Reader Commentary

Posted By:—on February 27, 2011
Congratulations. Your friend in words, Pete
[Request Review]

Posted By:—on February 27, 2011
Congratulations on this win.—Brandy :)
[Request Review]

Posted By:—on February 27, 2011
This poem is so tender and loving all the way through to the end. Life repeats itself over and over again. I hope this mother is as good as the other. Just beautiful and so moving. Great job.
[Request Review]

Posted By:—on February 27, 2011
Beautiful and touching poem. Congratulations. I am happy to share this win with you.—Rose
[Request Review]

Posted By:—on March 1,2011
Such a poignant story you tell here. Many times a son and his mother have ties stronger than any other in life…and the sadness when one passes is extreme, making one question the reasons. There are no real answers. We must just accept certain things and carry on. Beautifully written.—Lydi**
[Request Review]

Posted By:—on March 8, 2011
A great story you've developed here, so full of tenderness and deep love. I'm a single mom of four who raised three sons, so I know the unique relationship a mother has with her sons. Very heartfelt!—PDE
[Request Review]

Posted By:—on March 19, 2011
I was so touched by this piece. Truly touched. If it is a true story, I am even more impressed. This was such a lovely piece…some places I became tearful…I was captured by your words… Well written.
[Request Review]

Posted By:—on February 19, 2011
This made me get teary-eyed, such heartfelt and loving words. This is a priceless little gem. Thank you for sharing your tender thoughts with me.—Brandy:)
[Request Review]

Posted By: GUEST on February 19, 2011
It's always joyful when something I say is felt and moved it some way. We, poets, are always reaching out to express meaning words. When they work, we are extremely happy. I thank you for what you said.—Zishan
[Request Review]

Posted By:—on February 19, 2011
This touched my heart deeply. You write with such emotion. Very well done :)—Julie
[Request Review]

Posted By:—on February 20, 2011
Julie, thanks for your comment. I appreciate your words.—Zishan
[Request Review]

Posted By:—on February 21, 2011
This was a very touching and sad poem. Beautifully written! Good luck! Hugs, Terri
[Request Review]

Posted By:—on February 21, 2011
Mary T, your comment is appreciated. I am happy when my words moves someone to reply. Thank you.—Zishan
[Request Review]

Posted By:—on February 22,2011
This was such a tenderhearted write, surely tugged on my heart. I enjoyed it so much!—Pam :)
[Request Review]

Posted By:—on February 23,2011
Beautiful poem and sad to o
[Request Review]

Posted By:—on February 25, 2011
And the circle goes around and around, poignant write, sine.—Jean.
[Request Review]

Posted By:—on February 27, 2011
Congrats on your well-deserved win! I am happy to share the win with you!
Hugs, your friend, Terri
[Request Review]

Posted By:—on February 27, 2011
Congratulations

I KNOW MY LOVE IS WAITING

She doesn't know me yet.
She hasn't seen my face.
But she will.
When she does, I'll be her greatest thrill.
For sure, we'll hug and kiss and chat about
reasons why,
It took so very long to reach this lovely day.
It doesn't matter why, we need not rectify.
Here we are together holding hands,
Making plans.

I'm sure she's searching too.
And feel the way I do.
For one day we will meet
Join together
Form a bond
Knowing our love is warm.
And will stand any storm.

At night I go to bed.
And on the candlelight.
I see her with my eyes.
Wow! She is such a prize.

I can't sleep.
But I must,
To continue my quest.
Until she's here, I won't rest.

I picture her to be
A gem ready for me.
I'll travel anywhere
If I can find her there.
And tell her
How lovely
It is for us to bind
Lasting love all the time.

When I see her I'll stare.
I'll tell her, you're the one.
I'll hug her very tight
And whisper in her ear
Oh! God! She's finally here.

2011

FINALLY, MY CHANCE
HAS COME

Finally, my chance has come
I've asked the Lord above
To help me find my love.
Now I'm closer to where she is
I am sure she will appear.

Finally, my chance has come
Awake at morning time
Looking for love that's mine.
My sweet dreams always disappear.
But I'm certain she is near.

For sure, I can make my case.
I've prepared a word or two that's great.
It might just set a fire
Under the one I'm sure to admire.

Finally, my chance has come
Looking in my love's eyes
While she is at my side.
Now I know dreams really come true
Bringing joyfulness to you.

2010

SHE'S JUST THE PERFECT ONE FOR ME

She's just the perfect one for me.
Even though I wonder, where is she?
I know that she appears often in my dreams
And her absence is less than what it seems.

She's just the perfect one for me.
I would gladly give my all to see
Her beauty, her smile, and the color of her eyes,
Her wonderful way that always satisfies.

I often feel that she's within my sight.
And when I see her, I know things will be all
right.
Just to hold her hands and hug her tight
Will make my world a marvelous delight.

She's just the perfect one for me.
The one who'll fill my life with glee.
I am sure that many dreams come true
Bringing lots of love and happiness to you.

2010

PASSING TIME

Run, river, run
Make your waves in the hot sun.
Cool breeze blowing.
Happy faces are glowing.
Cheerful folks make their way
Enjoying a lovely day.

Holding hands
Sharing stories of the past,
Hoping enjoyment will last.
Smiling like playful little ones,
Giggling and having fun.

Looking back at years gone by
Still together as one.
As anniversaries come and go
Holding on to what they know.

2010

ABOUT LOVE XI

Taking A chance when romance is on your plate?
When all goes bad,
You change your mate.
Don't linger. It only increases your pain.
Move on!
Other suitors are willing to make your call.
Although true, lasting love is in short supply.
There are some. You can fine love if you try.
Love you and share that love with those you care.
Scrutinize before you commit.
Make sure the one you choose is the one you get.
Also, the lifestyle and faith are what you feel.
True lasting love you can surely find.
If you are careful, and take the time.

2011

ABOUT LOVE XII

(From: Thoughts on Love l-XX)

Love can be bittersweet.
It can be one sided.
It can be for convenience.
Temporary at best.
Should one hang on or cut bait,
And head for the gate?
If you are not number one,
You are two, three,
Maybe four.
If staying get you that,
Head for the door.
You are better than that.
Be a magnet for the best.
Leave the rest.
Your heart will recover.
You will be better for it.
Go with the truth.
If it's not in your best interest,
Cut it *loose*.

2011

ABOUT LOVE XIII

It's pain ful being the other woman.
Your lover comes and rushes away.
He has a permanent love life,
And only comes to play.
He leaves you emotional,
Wishing he would stay.
Would you rather be the other woman,
Or the woman he has every day?
Are you worth more than a few minutes?
Do you love you at all?
There is not a shortage of love.
But true love, there is not as much.
But you can get true love if you try.
You must have confidence and believe in you.
Love yourself and share that love
With the good folks you know.
This will put you on a path
That will lead you to a true love
That will last.

2011

ABOUT LOVE XIV

You are drowning in love.
Your spellbound heart is
Overwhelmed by the precious one.
You are seeking a lasting love.
You have devised a plan,
For precious to consume
And give you her hand.
There is very little left for you to say,
To swoop that lovely lady your way.
Now! It's up to her to take it in.
To let you know when.
A wonderful romance will begin.

2011

ABOUT LOVE XV

Happiness comes when the heart is aroused,
By a lover hanging around.
Not the one who passed you by.
That's the one who made you cry.
Why waste a tear,
When the end is clear?
A true lover is waiting to snatch you.
It takes a little movement on your part.
Reach out and make a new start.
Love is always a risk.
You are wondering, will romance ever last?
It does, sometimes, but often not.
You can't change that.
The most you can do,
Is to be you.
Drown yourself in love for you
And those close ones too.
You must reach in and maintain your strength.
Until that true lover slips into your tent.

2011

ABOUT LOVE XVI

It is not fair to submit and give all you can,
When the one you love is an unfaithful man.
But life isn't fair.
And most lovers aren't either.
There are some, trustworthy and true
Willing to live a lifetime with you.
Should you make plans,
To find that faithful man?
If you want to, you surely can.
To romance that true man
You must circulate among those
With a lifestyle you like,
And a faith
You can relate.
These are the things you must do.
If a good man is to gravitate to you.

2011

ABOUT LOVE XVII

There is a time you know the end has come.
You open the gate and run.
No time to linger and puncture the heart.
It's time to move on for a new start.
Romance, often, is not for sure.
It starts good but ends bad.
Many times, you've been had.
Now what should you do?
Live your life free
Or seek one that's new.
If you want lasting love,
There are things you must do.
You can't be quick.
You will wind up in the same fix.
Take your time and scrutinize.
Make sure the one you pick
Is the one that fit,
With honesty and reachable goals.
This want guarantees you a love that last.
You may have a better fortune
Than you had in the past.

2011

ABOUT LOVE XVIII

Get up, girl!
There's a lot of excitement out there.
Waiting for you to make your move.
That will put you in a better groove.
No need to withdraw and pine.
There are good things for your mind.
Get with the happy folks,
Waiting for your time.
They will plant joy and happiness in your way,
Guaranteed to make an eventful day.
Move about with these folks that make you feel
That life is worth living and true love is real.
Then you'll jump for joy and holler a cheer.
Oh my god! I love it here.

2011

ABOUT LOVE XIX

The blame game disturbs the heart.
It tears lovers apart.
Who is to blame?
Both answers are usually the same,
It is always you.
Oh! If you could erase that pronoun.
But you can't.
There are things you can do.
You must be smart,
Before the romance start.
Scrutinize before you render your heart.
Make sure the one that you pick,
Shares your faith and lifestyle too.
Loving commitment must be your stand,
If that special one is to be your plan.
This want guarantee what you seek.
But it surely will let you have
A good night sleep.
Now you know things to do
To bring that happiness back to you.

2011

ABOUT LOVE XX

Let your dream continue,
Never let it go.
That utopian world is better
Than the world you know.
Life may be happier
When you merge fantasy
With the world that is.
But never lose sight
Of the love,
That living folk give.

2011

Zorta Evans

WOMEN

(A bit of humor)

There's a lot about a woman I don't understand.
No bother, I'm just a man.
Women put us in our place,
Especially when romance is on the plate.
She holds back when she chooses and make
us wait.
We even have to keep our fingers cross to get
a lovely date.
Now who do you suppose controls the heart
When a love affair is about to start?
Since it isn't me,
It must be she.
What other things a woman can claim
That brings an aggressive man to shame?
Holding back!
Don't give him a crack!
At that beautiful, magnetic love we possess,
Destroying an *ego* and caring less.

2011

THE SHADOW ON THE WALL

SHE IS NOT HERE.
IT'S BEEN A LONG TIME,
Since her shadow moved
About on my wall.
It would accelerate,
All the feelings within me.
I knew when it appeared,
She was near.

THE MEMORY, the way it was,
Never leaves.
We would snuggle up,
Smile, kiss,
And we drew closer for a while.
We were very happy.
We truly loved each other.
THEN what went wrong?
Only the one above knows.

BUT I DO KNOW.
One evening the shadow
Did not appear.
I am not sure why.
It just didn't.
I said to myself,
It will return tomorrow.
THAT tomorrow never came.
Weeks went by,
Months too.
I miss the love
I believed was true.

ONE DAY,
I looked up and saw
A shadow on my wall.
A smiled covered my face.
I opened my door.
The shadow was no more.
Shadows come and go.
But it's not my lover I see.
Oh! Shadow on my wall!

THE LAST KISS

We hugged and kissed with a passionate grip,
As though our romance would never slip.
Like many whose fire has quickly waned
And left a hole filled with pain.
We said goodbye and released our arms,
Planted a kiss to last till dawn.
Went a separate way
Till the end of the day.

I looked everywhere and could not see
The one who shared a life with me.
The day passed, weeks and months too.
I wondered what I should do.

Searching and searching with little results to
show
Where my love could be
To bring her back to me.

It's been years now,
I have suffered endless grief.
I remember that kiss
And the love that never cease.

WHEN THERE IS NO YOU

A tear is falling from my eye,
Dripping, dripping, dripping as I cry.
I can't help but whisper her name,
To drown the sorrow and reduce the pain.

There aren't happy songs to sing,
When all my moves are a losing game.
Withdrawn from the ways our pleasure was,
Changing the thoughts of an endearing love.

The beautiful memories of the past,
The wonderful dreams that didn't last.
Oh! Life of mine return to the old,
And bring her back to heal my soul.

2010

A MOMENT IN THE SUN

The steady raindrops clung to her hair,
She did not bring a hat to wear.
She chose to feel the rain,
And let it splash on her face,
To disguise her tears in a secluded place.
The rain made her feel surrounded and free,
Away from trouble she always sees.
She wishes rain would not cease,
And allow the spirits release.
Suddenly, the sun sent its rays down,
It made her face turn into frowns.
Sad thoughts would now begin,
Of the love that had to end.
Soon dark clouds came around,
Rain begin to reappear,
Bringing memories of one so dear.
Ah! The rain cleansed her so,
Made her free to let love go.

2011

THE WIND

Standing alone,
The wind has come and gone.
My only love is blown away.
The pain gets heavy each day.
I felt wind slashing my face.
It moves with uncertain grace.
Bringing thoughts of one who left fast.
Leaving all the thrills to the past.
Watery eyes and desperation too,
Chasing everywhere just for you.
I shout to the wind, please, blow you here,
And take away all my fear.
You're the only one I see,
Bringing joy to you and me.

WHEN WILL I CLAIM
THE ONE FOR ME

It seems like I've reached the end of the road.
Nothing has happened to soothe my soul.
There is one for me somewhere.
I long to be right there.

The days pass, the weeks too.
Even though I search, still there is no you.
I go to bed every night,
Hoping my love appear in my sight.

Ah! Those sweet songs the birds sing.
The joyous love call they bring.
I wait for that special day to come,
When someone brings to me lasting love.

2012

WHY ME

I keep asking myself, "What is life all about?"
"What is left when love moves away,
Besides pain, agony, and blues every day?"
"Why have things been so mean,
Destroying every meaningful dream?"

Caught up in faith and hope,
It seems like I'm just a dope.
I'm missing something, but I don't know what.
Maybe, the way it is, is how it's supposed to be.
And just maybe, this is all that's left for me.

There is a place, the Good Book says, over there.
Where love and happiness are everywhere.
Let me try to make it here,
Reach out and claim my dear.

I know it might not be.
But oh! I have to chance it just to see.

2010

"WHERE HAS ROMANCE GONE"

The TV is blasting away,
With lovers having their say.
It's such a lovely, romantic game,
Everyone wish to experience the same.
Oh! Romance! Where are you today?
You have decided to duck my way.
You have stopped without leaving a trail,
Making sure my attempt surely fail.
I don't know why I'm punish so much,
I've been good, I'm a soft touch.
Then again, maybe I'm not.
Could it be just my charades?
My heart is still running nonstop.
I'm always open to anything,
That brings romance my way.
Although I have my doubts,
I think romance will come, anyway.

2011

MY FRIEND

There is a precious friend that's far away.
I can't see her every day.
I talk to her in many ways.
Cherishing every word she says.

She's such a joyful and pleasant gem.
Often she looks petite and trim.
I like the way she hugs her friend.
It's like a love that has no end.

I miss her when our chatter cease.
And in my mind there's little peace.
Until those hearten words appear.
In my head as though she is near.

2010

THE END OF A SEASON

From the womb emerged a future voice.
Ten years later a phenomenal resource.
Formal education and contact sports,
Brought an outstanding academic report.
Higher degree and beautiful girls,
Never blurred the focus on a changing world.
Head up high and chest standing tall,
An accomplished force in a world in turmoil.
Wife and kids and many cherished friends,
Religious ceremony all would attend.
Kids grow up as everyone knows,
Grandchildren come knocking at the door.
Always proud of a large family group,
Life has been good to an amazing troop.
Suddenly, sickness invades the cherished space,
A sense of helplessness caused an emergency embrace.
As calamity creeps violently upon the bed,
It takes its toll till all are dead.

2010

WHEN LOVE MOVES AWAY

It is not easy when love moves away,
You cry and grieve, many days.
Love is by choice,
You can't change that.
But you can love you,
And the things you do.
Love is everywhere,
You can get it if you try.
Reach out and mingle with the folks that
make you feel,
Life is worth living and lasting love is real.
To lose a love open the way,
To that true love that will stay.

2011

SEARCHING FOR LOVE

She was all he had,
Never wanting anymore.
Even though she slammed the door,
All the memories made him glad.
Still searching everywhere
And looking here and there,
Sure to revive love anew
Although there never was a clue.
Trying and trying,
Hoping to find a way.
Dreaming, seeking for anything
That would stop the need for crying.
It's true, life will have its pain,
Wishing love will return again.

WHEN LOVE GOES BAD

To stick or split,
A hard choice to make.
But you must.
After plunging into a romantic affair
With love and happiness always there,
It's hard to consider love will fail.
But with vivid signs, you could tell,
Something wrong was really there.
A shock, a blow entered your space.
What type of action you should take?
Questions pound in your head.
Should you let it end this way?
Or pull back and hope it goes away?
Love is everywhere.
The end is not the end.
It's the beginning,
A search for a better friend.
More often than not, it happens.
You dry up your tears.
Joy is back in your plan.
For sure, you can claim a loving man.

2011

LOVE IS FOR ALWAYS

(Woe of a Dear Friend)

My call to the Most High is in vain.
Yearnings for a savior still remain.
The answer, to my sorrow, is not there.
My pain is unbearable, who will care?
Death lurking at the window and the moon.
The end is certain to come very soon.
With endless nights and sad, lonely days,
A miserable life is on the wane.
Time passes, and I don't know what to do.
As death makes its call, I think of you.
And in my misery, I am with glee,
Because of the love you shared with me.

2010

I HAD YOU IN MY ARMS

I had you in my arms.
You gave me a second chance,
I turned away from your love.
You left me, and now I'm in a trance.
I cry at night because you are not here.
When will this pain go away?
How can I make amends?

I left, you ran away.
I don't know the price to pay
To capture the love that's in your heart,
And return to days we weren't apart.
Darling, life is not the same.
I'm through with playing games.

Forgive me,
And give me another chance.
Forgive me for what I was,
I'm not the fool anymore.
Forgive me,
And claim what we missed in the past.
Forgive me,
I'll make up for the lost we had.

I let go for others,
And now you are with another.
I can't imagine you are away,
I hope and pray that you will come one day.
Please, darling, return to me,
And I will never stray!

WHEN ALL EFFORTS FAIL

The moon is not so bright,
It's glowing with very little light.
The night is shutting down,
Day is coming around.
Before it does, there is a buzz,
All over this place.
Where! Oh, where is my love!

My mind is full of pain,
What did I do to bring this shame?
I know I wasn't always there,
To hold your hand to show I care.
But I was always true,
All my love was spent on you.

When I awake, you are not here.
Emptiness is my greatest fear.
Since you are gone away from me,
Just your picture is all I see.

I look for you each day,
But, no, you, come my way.
Come, girl, why aren't you here?
Although I search, you don't appear.

2011

SHE'S GONE

Ah! Those happy days of the past,
The joy that wouldn't last.
Caught up in a lonely way,
Never thought she would stray.
Even though I love her so,
I had no choice but to see her go.
Oh! That lonely road we travel,
Has pitfalls along the way.
When you think you're going straight,
A fork comes in to play.
It doesn't matter how far you stray,
There is no perfect route to take.
Love sometimes veers along the way,
When hearts are broken you must pay.
The heart tell us what we should do,
With love in our heart, always be true.

2011

61

UNWANTED

(A foster Child)

I'm punished.
For what?
I don't really know.
I suffer the fate of an unwanted child.
I was tossed in the world.
Put in a nameless pile.
No one seemed to care.
The burden I had to bare.
I had few choices.
My fate was sealed.
I should cry.
But what will it yield?

2011

ON FEAR

Lonely as the darkness falls,
And the moon is piercing bright.
Stars are traveling everywhere,
As shadows surrounds the night.

Constantly, I look for solace,
While pursuing a better way.
To retreat from hardships and pain,
Doubtful of what tomorrow will bring.

Walking steady and guided by artificial lights,
Looking everywhere to escape the morbid
sights,
That transcend everything we hold so dear.
But if we dwell on the pitfalls,
We'll surely surrender to fear.

2011

THE GOOD AND THE BAD

Here we are, the good and the bad,
Sharing the same fate that we try to understand.
Now is it possible to overcome our plight,
When confusion and death appear in our
sight?

Everyone suffers by dead or by chance,
Those who believe and those who don't.
The good cry out for deliverance and fail,
The bad, causing mayhem, strive to prevail.

Life is confusing with pain and sorrow,
Some have no choice, others do.
The fate of many are in the hands of a few,
Is this the will of a creator, or will we know
tomorrow?

Oh! Heavenly one! Save us from our fears,
And give us a sign that you are real.

2010

A PATH TO LOVE

Love has made its way to my life.
Can I be sure it's all right?
Will my life be free of strife,
While my world is celestial bright?
Must I cling to the belief in sight?
There might not be a second chance.
Tackle it with all my night,
As I travel this road to romance.
One day I will surely reach that place,
Where all doubts has no meaning.
All the fears will be erased,
With my love always clinging.
The most I can hope for is to make,
A choice that's true and not a mistake.

2011

SEARCHING FOR WORDS

I'm filled with amorous desire,
My fragile heart is on fire.
The one for me usually comes my way,
I believe one day she will stay.

I imagine how life would be,
With the lover that's meant for me.
Even though I see her at day,
I haven't found the right words to say.

My heart accelerates when she is near,
I always wish she comes right here.
Somehow I'll gain strength to say words I feel,
Letting her know my love is real.

When I do, I'm sure she will come to me,
Bringing happiness, everyone will see.

2012

UNCONDITIONAL LOVE

Unconditional love is hard to find,
It's elusive most of the time.
You look within and see what's not,
Hanging on, hoping love want stop.
Wishing the things you do will say,
You are you with your wonderful way.

LOOKING BACK

Will you love me always, not let me go?
Can our love continue and travel on?
If the wind blow you away, you'll never show.
When our childhood leave us, will you be gone?
I cry sometimes while enjoying our love.
My dreams are filled with thoughts and passion too.
Hoping a smile comes from heaven above.
All because of the love I have for you.
Why do young folks suddenly fall in love?
Is this the fate one carry to the grave,
Romance that has precious enjoyment of?
Can we get around this emotional slave?
Even though this period of time is not all,
The love we had or have is never small.

2012

THE LAST WORDS

We laugh, played, sang soulful songs,
That touched our hearts while moving along,
Beautiful lyrics filled our minds,
We hummed and smiled a long time.
The destination we chose to go,
Was a place true lovers know.
We spent lots of time sharing thoughts,
Hugging, kissing, moving about.
The day hurried to come to an end,
A move toward our abode began.
The last words before going our separate way,
"I LOVE YOU" is all we could say.
There isn't any happy songs left to sing,
Until my love comes back again.

2012

A LOVER'S PRAYER

I don't know what to say without you.
I'm not myself when you are away.
Often I wonder what I should do.
When you are near, it's a happy day.
You have devoured me with your spell.
Our caring brings fulfillment to each.
The feeling in my heart, you can tell.
The depth of love is beyond reach.
Oh my lord! Tell her I love her so.
Loving her is for always, my sweet.
Say to her, I will never let her go.
I am at peace, my life is complete.
Lord, after our life on earth ends,
Bring us back together again.

2012

A LOVER'S CRY

Why did you say you love me,
And later tell me goodbye?
How could you hold my hand,
Let it go and never return again?

You have destroyed the happiness that was,
For another untried love.
I must let you go,
Because you have shut the door.

Oh! What have I done so bad,
To make my life hopeless and sad?
I've led a simple life.
I did my best,
To share love with all in sight.

There is something missing,
And I don't know what to do.
Therefore, I'm saying this prayer because of
you.
Lord, send me peace and relieve my pain,
So I can have happiness once again.

ALMIG

(A Person We Care About)

Almig, with a smile, was a moment of joy. A simple pleasure all of us hoped for. Almig was a dreamer traveling an uncharted course throughout her complex existence. She was not easy to define but surely one of God's children. We all loved her dearly even though we could never completely enter her world, a world that sometimes seems afar off. But suddenly, like a thunderbolt, although momentarily, her lovely side would appear, bringing a sense of happiness to all of us. We hoped, for a day uncertain, that this lovely person would one day reclaim her place in this changing world. Our hopes and prayers for Almig were continuous without pause. Oh! How we loved and cared for this unique traveler who has moved to that special place we all pray and hope for. Goodbye, oh beautiful dreamer, we will never forget you and never stop loving you, "our dear Almig."

THREE LITTLE BIRDS

There are three little birds that sing and play.
They are sometimes friends but fight all day.
These birds sing like they want to flee.
From a cage that house them, permanently.

Chewing on the cage and trying to bite through steel.
Disappointed the poor birds in every way.
Is claustrophobia an emotion that these birds feel?
Have mercy on the poor bird held against their will.

2010

AT THE WINDOW

Passing by, stopping now and then,
I wonder what's in their head.
Going their way, a new day begins,
As I lie in my cozy bed.
Their faces say many things,
That must come as they reach their place.
It's hard to figure the changes,
That settle in a working state.
This routine happens day by day,
I see this as a revolving door.
When the end comes, they pass my way,
It always ends like before.
Oh! If this is the life they mean,
May by happiness lies in between.

2012

ARMS

The arms attached to the shoulders,
Extending as far as they can reach.
Surrounding all that yearn great joy,
Especially the soul mate one savor.

For sure arms are very meaningful,
A mighty, caring, precious savior.
Holding one who is full of pain,
Giving hope and peace to sustain.

Without the arms, what would life be?
How could we squeeze the one we love,
The one we cling to with passion,
And share the unlimited love from above?

Humbly, let's pray these arms will stay,
To help us navigate through life each day.

THIS IS A GLORIOUS DAY TO BEGIN

As I travel on my journey away from it all,
I stop and stare, I hear your voice.
I give in to your call.
With you, love is all I can see.
This is a glorious day to begin.
I pray that our love will never end.

As I travel on my journey this lovely day,
I marvel at your beauty and the sweetness of
your way.
Who knows the effect of this meeting on our
desire,
The change in our expectation and our
satisfier.
This is a glorious day to begin.
I pray that our love will never end.

The wisdom of our meeting is so divine.
The vision of our world is sweet as wine.
The meaning of our lives, I cannot tell.
The extent of our love is more than a spell.

As I travel on my journey with you at my side,
I hear the melodies of the robin, the wind, and
the tide.
The cause of our meeting is a heavenly thing.
The thrust of our passion, I cannot restrain.
This is a glorious day to begin.
I pray that our love will never end.

2010

WAITING AROUND

I'm always glad when you smile.
And hold my hand for a while.
You make my day full of glee.
Bringing joy to you and me.
I open up my heart to you.
Letting you know I'm always true.
From you I cannot escape.
Or my heart will surely break.
I wait patiently each day.
When you suddenly appear, my heart silently
cheer.
Then I call you by your name.
Your heavenly response is always the same.

2010

FOREVER MY LOVE

The roses are blooming,
Spring is in the air.
My love is meeting me,
At the county fair.
Ferris wheel, rides,
Hot dogs, and popcorn too.
A lovely day with
Wonderful things to do.
Circulating around,
Eating and winning,
Prizes everywhere.
Chatting and laughing,
All through the day.
Hugging, kissing,
And loving play.
The shadows of night
Came strolling by
As we walked holding hands
Saying beautiful love words
Both could understand.

She whispered in my ear,
"Do you love me
And care in every way?"
Forever, my love,
With you I'll always stay.

THE FEELING WITHIN

*

No words can describe the overwhelming
Desire you bring to me.
That feeling captures every emotion
And creates happiness all can see.
Life has changed.
Comfort ensues, leading
The way to complete euphoria.
No one but you have the key
That open that door to my fragile heart.
You swell the eyes of many
But romance only me.
Our destiny is a life sweet and harmonious.
Together we will prevail over all obstacle.
You bring fulfillment to our world.
You are the one all hope for.
We have made our choice.
I have found the cure to my cravings, YOU.

2010
HAPPY VALENTINE'S DAY!

OUR KIDS

Mom and Dad

Losers or gainers,
Who can say?
We hope the sun
Is bright every day.
Track and field
Volleyball too
Don't forget football
That guy would do.
Winners is the joy we often had,
But now gloom hovers
Over our head.
Is this what the Evans and Cooglers
Looked for all these years.
Or are we seeing something
That spikes our fears?
Two families giving up their
Pride and joy.
Bound together like lovers do
Making one out of two.

"Hallelujah!" the families shout.
A union both families grew happy about.
Best wishes and a lot of love.
Surround the couple
As they travel on their way
Joyfully all would say.
Suddenly a toast by all

Near and far for the family's star.
Everyone gathered around
Hollering cheers
As Zinzi and Ryan travel on a honeymoon
that will last for years.

2016

AT CHRISTMAS

Christmas day is on the way.
Bringing happiness and cheer.
Folks everywhere always say.
It's the best time of the year.
Ho! Ho! Ho! and a lot more.
Santa makes his way to each door.
"Here are toys," he called to Mom and Dad.
Give them to the good children you had.
Out in the snow Santa went.
To another house he was sent.
Happy faces stormed the room.
Their holiday wishes will be open soon.
Laughter and play was the mood.
While the family expressed their gratitude.

WHERE DID MY NEIGHBOR GO

I saw him every day across my fence,
A busy, retired, jolly gent.
He looked happy with big smiles,
During the early morning hours.
His beautiful yard was covered with grass,
Lots of flowers and fruit trees too.
Loved flowers, he told me so,
Shared the fruit that always grow.

I liked that guy,
He always had good things to say.
I watched him in his yard every day,
Prayed happiness would stay his way.
One day, I looked over my fence,
My neighbor was not there.
I said to myself, he's only gone for a while,
He'll be back with that big smile.
I'm sure to see him tomorrow, I said,
Late that night when I went to bed.

The weeks past, he did not appear.
I start asking the people near,
No one new or could give me a clue.
I start worrying, what should I do?
After inquiring everywhere,
this is what I found.
My neighbor has moved to another town.
Now I can't say that is true.
I do know I miss my neighbor.
He was always a blessing to you.

2011

TROUBLE IN PARADISE

It was in high school, Alice and John became
best friends.
They said their love would never end.
Alice and John had the blessings of their parents.
It was for everything, except making love.

The couple had a lot of love and respect for
their parents.
They held to their wishes as long as they could.
Overwhelmed by the love within,
Celibacy was hard to defend.

Off to college, together they went.
Two families were filled with happiness.
At the party filled with family and friends,
They shared two rings, an engagement began.

The college graduates went to work in their
fields.
Marriage came quickly.
Family and friends filled the church.
After reception and gifts,
On a honeymoon they went.

Time past.
Two loving kids brought joy in their lives.
Here was a loving couple, admired by all,
Living in paradise.

Alice and John were happy and successful.
John was a great dad and husband.
Alice was the perfect wife.
Both were excited with the jobs they held.

It was announced at the office and on bulletin boards,
That John was promoted to a higher position.
There was a lot of excitement at the office.
Coworkers were overjoyed.

John's wife was away, for a day, on a job assignment.
Their two kids were at home with the babysitter.
Everyone at the office agreed,
A celebration at the club was the place to be.
Work came to a halt, to the club they went.

John and the group gathered at the club.
It was a place where enjoyment begin.
Drinking, dancing, toasting, eating,
And sharing humorous thoughts.
A joyful party that seemed to never end.

It was very late, John was not his usual self.
It appeared the drinking took its toll.
"I should take you home," she said.
"You certainly can't navigate your way."
"Hold on to me," she said. "'Til I take you in
my car."

Off they went.
John held on to her while she open her door.
They went in, she led him to her bed.
He lay down for the night.

The sun finally arrived.
John jumped up from the bed.
He noticed he had no clothes on,
His companion was naked too.
Panic set in.
John realized he must get home quickly,
To prepare for work and say goodbye to his kids.

John rushed home after work.
He greeted his loving wife.
She had returned from her work assignment.
They kissed, shared happy thoughts, and played with the kids.
They were happy with each other.
They put their kids to bed.
Lovemaking was in their head.

Several day past.

John experienced unusual feelings that disturbed him.

They were intense.

John went to his physician, friend, for evaluation.

The bad news brought fright to John's face.

The doctor said, "What YOU have I can cure."

"It's VD."

John cried out in a loud voice,
"What about my wife!"

2012

ABOUT LOVE I

Love comes whether you are ready or not.
It's an uncontrollable force,
That pierces the heart and captures the mind.
Love can be rewarding or pain,
When another doesn't feel the same.
Love is everywhere.
But elusive when sinking a bait,
You pull it in or you have to wait.

2010

ABOUT LOVE II

Love is risk but profound.
It provides the passion,
That soothe the mind and accelerates the heart.
Love creates a climate for intimate ecstasy,
Beyond description.
Love, whether short or long,
Has moments of sheer magic,
Where the mind wanders,
In an indescribable euphoria,
Drifting in union and endless pleasure.

2010

ABOUT LOVE III

When love strikes, you succumb.
You are caught up and can't run.
Your will is sunk.
You submit with uncontrollable desire.
Your whole body is on fire.
Giving in is all you want.
Let the passion begin.
Lovemaking without end.

2010

ABOUT LOVE IV

It is not easy when love runs away.
You cry and grieve with few words to say.
It tears the heart and bruise the mind.
Those pleasant days are no more.
When ecstasy you had fled your door.
Oh! That love you dreamed of let you down.
Left lingering pain, all around.

2011

ABOUT LOVE V

After many good years,
With a spouse and sweat,
Your kids grew up,
They did their very best.
Suddenly you lost your grip,
On the happiness you had.
Threw up your hands,
As love pass.
No more together,
With passion in your step.
It's over,
You gently wept.

2011

ABOUT LOVE VI

That budding romance filled your day,
With only hearten words to say.
Passion and euphoria consumed your mind,
With thoughts of lovemaking all the time.
Your heart is full of endless joy,
The one you love is at your side.
Dreamland is where you reside.

2010

ABOUT LOVE VII

True love depends on you,
And others
Who enjoy the things you do.
Love is risky without guarantees.
If you are sincere
And share faith and goals alike,
You are doing things right.
When you do, the chance is good,
The love you choose
Will be a lasting love for you.

2011

ABOUT LOVE VIII

Mesmerized, overpowered, consumed,
Bound together with passion that sticks.
This is the reason you care to mix.
Bodies caressing, tightly fixed,
Eyes reaching into space.
Hands go wild in a trail,
Neither one cares
Under this ecstatic spell.

2011

ABOUT LOVE IX

Love must come freely,
A choice of the heart.
Two lovers must bind,
Without remorse.
They look at each other,
Day by day.
Ah! The beautiful words they say.
They laugh and play, giggle too,
Loving the many things they do.
This is true love.
Nothing else will do.
If love is not this way,
It must go.
For sure,
The love you wish for
Will show.

2011

ABOUT LOVE X

Happiness seldom appears,
When romance fades away.
Life becomes stressful,
It seems like every day.
It's hard to shake loose, what was,
And move on to ways of finding a new love.
A love that stays,
And not run away.
You can.
But scrutiny must be in your plan,
You have a lot of love to share.
Make sure the one you choose,
Is that special one for you.
Lifestyle and faith is important too.
Your quest will improve,
Finding the true love for you.

2011

SCARS

They hugged and kissed,
Two loving married folks.
Today was like most days when they awoke.
Their eyes touched,
Conveying loving feeling.
Although there were things
They were concealing.
Passionate words were spoken,
All they can.
They parted for work,
With a dinner plan.
Jane's coworker kissed her
At her desk,
Surrounded with flowers
And picturesque.
Tom stopped with his coworker
For breakfast.
Enjoying every moment
While it last.
Tom loved Jane, and she loved him.
They enjoyed being together.
It was at bedtime, guilt appeared.
Pass quickly as it occurred.

A busy life they had
Since they had
High-level positions,
Kept in touch in all the conditions.
Tom and several executives

Left for five-day project.
Among them was Tom's coworker.
After work they would connect,
It was at the club.
Jane and coworker had a lovely time.
Coworker was sober,
Decided to drive her for bedtime.
Coworker drove Jane to her house,
Both fell asleep until day.
Coworker smiled at Jane,
At daybreak dressed and went away.
Tom returned, hugged, and kissed,
Went to dinner filled with passion deep.
They returned home,
And did what true lovers do
Then went to sleep.

2016

MY THOUGHTS

Those old days,
Oh, how beautiful those old days were.
No worry, no bother, just fun and love,
You wish you could go back to those playful
days.
Night was a bother, you hated when it came,
Couldn't wait for the day to do your thing.
Friends were in abundance,
They came from everywhere.
You played jacks, jumped rope, and other
games too.
When it came to parties, they always invited
you.
Now here you are looking back in time.
It's good to think of those earlier days.
But sorry they won't come your way.
You have to move straight ahead,
And dream of that old happiness
When you go to bed.

2011

When love wanes, the music stops.
Life takes on a losing game.
Romance is not the same.
What's left is only pain.
Love is everywhere.
More than you need.
But true love is not.
If love doesn't fit,
Get rid of it.
If you scrutinize with care,
You can win.
You may get the one you want,
In the end.

2011

MY THOUGHTS NO. 3

True love is a prize.
Desired by many, receive by some.
Those who have it share a happy life.
Those who don't, hope they might.
True love is available, the result of scrutiny.
Be careful always with those you see.
Mingle with others with high standards and views to match.
Love yourself and share that love with those you care.
There is an abundance of love.
It's everywhere, have confidence.
Believe in you and others will too.

MY THOUGHTS NO. 4

To put aside a love, that is not true, is not easy.
It wounds the heart and may tarnish the mind.
But it must happen.
Lingering only perpetuates the pain.
You can move on to a true love.
There are some true lovers out there.
They are not easy to find, but you can.
You must take extra care and scrutinize before
you bind.
Make sure the faith and lifestyle is what you
care.
Mingle with those who share your views.
Then you'll have a better person to choose.

2011

MY THOUGHTS NO. 5

You can't change the past,
Neither can you erase the bad.
All the pain and suffering you caused,
Will linger forever in your mind.
And only gradually submerge with passing time,
Should you pine and wine or move on.
Look at the past as things to learn.
Your life can be better in time.
Make improvements day by day.
Your shame may gradually go away.

2011

MY THOUGHTS NO. 6

A broken heart can be healed.
It will fly away if that's your will.
If you look beyond the pain,
There is love for you to gain.
You have folks who love you so,
Who'll lift you when your spirit is low.
Don't dwell on the hurt and strain,
Think of all the love friends bring.
Good folks are here to cheer your day,
So happiness will come your way.

2011

MY THOUGHTS NO. 7

We make up the world.
The world is constantly changing.
Whatever it is, we are part of the blame.
We can stand aside and have our say.
But there will not be a better day.
Unless we change our way.
Greed and power is on the plate.
Love has little chance because of hate.
Why bother! What can we do?
We are just a speck in the land.
So was Christ, Gandhi, and Martin Luther
King too.
The change depends on you.
Every voice has a place.
Yours is one.
That's what it takes.

2011

MY THOUGHTS NO. 8

We are not born faithful,
We learn it.
The urge for another is pervasive.
If we hold on to what we know,
One is the way to go.
Control! Heaven knows it's not easy.
Hearts can move back and forth with risk.
We are the judge.
Maintain peace and harmony,
Or travel to the emotional brings.

MY THOUGHTS NO. 9

You have what it takes to navigate,
Through this worldly maze.
You are strong even though you complain.
You fulfill your day.
You deserve more but get less.
The Good Book says God is Love.
And God loves you.
Even though it seems it isn't true.
Continue the good things you do.
So when life is through,
Heaven will be waiting for you.

2011

MY THOUGHTS NO. 10

Little kids' eyes full of joy.
Great America's rides.
Fun and frolic, ice cream,
And sweets that's nice.
Mom watches, sometimes with dad,
Keeping everyone in sight.
Grown folks are too consumed
With money and fame
To be bothered with children games.
So the world sinks while many
Cry out for help.
Ignored by the comfortable few,
Who think only of themselves.

MY THOUGHTS NO. 11

Pain is not a happy thing,
It's everywhere.
Some seldom change,
But YOU can.
It last as long as you let it stand.
You must make the move,
The other party is causing you to lose.
The very thing you hold so dear,
Your will to choose.
Love is pervasive and always there.
However there are heartrending
Things you must do,
To make a better life for you.

MY THOUGHTS NO. 12

Why cry over love that walked away,
When a true love stands waiting to come your way.
Love is risky,
No proof it stays.
You only hope it last, always.
When it's gone, it's gone.
Don't pout! Move on!
If a lasting love is what you seek,
Take care and don't be quick.
Be sure of one's truthful before you pick,
Also a faith you can share.
The goals and lifestyle must fit,
While one brings happiness that will never quit.

MY THOUGHTS NO. 13

It's time to change,
To make a move for better things.
To some, love is a game,
It doesn't matter who suffer the pain.
When the writing is on the wall,
It's not the time to stall.
Get going!
There is someone out there for you,
It depends on what you do.
Love is all over the place,
But take care before you date.
Make sure the quality you admire
Appears in the lover that you require.

MY THOUGHTS NO. 14

To awake every day of the week,
Is a blessing we seek.
We can thank the mighty *one* above,
For showering us with unlimited love.
When we spread our *love* in many ways,
We are following the messages
The *Good Book* says.

MY THOUGHTS NO. 15

To be in a romantic love affair is very neat.
Your search is over, your love is complete.
You have accomplished what so many
Wished they had.
Your concern now is to make it last.
That can happen.
It seldom does.
You have determine to try.
And hope your love will never die.
So if you put the effort in,
Your love may last and never end.

MY THOUGHTS NO. 16

You are completely overwhelm and rightly so.
There is a guy in your place that's *wow*.
He has the style that makes you faint.
Snug in his arms like he's your saint.
There are so many words you could say.
But you let your feelings have its way.
This is what life is overwhelming about.
Making love that make you move and shout.
On cloud nine and in bliss.
Exploring exciting touches and kiss.
There is no limit to where this will go.
You'll play it by ear and let love flow.
And when the days finally end.
Tomorrow you'll start all over again.

MY THOUGHTS NO. 17

Oh! What a wonderful thought,
To go back in time.
To clean the mess you left behind.
Sorry! It won't happen.
However there are other things you can do.
To block out the past,
Find a true love that will last.
That you can.
It's in your hand.
Take your time, scrutinize with care.
You seldom lose.
Chances are good,
You'll get the one you choose.

MY THOUGHTS NO. 18

To stick or split,
A hard choice to make.
But you must.
After plunging into a romantic affair,
With love and happiness always there.
It's hard to consider love will fail.
But with vivid signs, you could tell.
Something wrong was really there.
A shock a blow interred your space.
What course of action should you take?
Questions pound in your head.
Should you let it end this way,
Or pull back and hope it goes away?
Your call is crucial.
Love is everywhere,
The end is not the end.
It's the beginning of the search for a better friend.
More often than not it happens.
So dry up your tears and put joy back in your plan.
Will you find the true love that last?
For sure, yes, you can.

MY THOUGHTS NO. 19

He's wanting you,
Whenever the wind begin to blow.
I open my window wide,
Hoping it carries her inside.
I miss the moments love was here,
But now she is never near.
It doesn't matter where she be,
Her presence I always see.
Every day the sweat continuously flows,
When the image of her comes and goes.
Can't change the demons of the past,
I'm still hoping for a love that last.

MY THOUGHTS NO. 20

True love doesn't come easy,
It can be the luck of the draw.
Romance is risky,
An encounter with maybe yes or maybe no.
Then where should you go,
To improve your chances for lasting true love?
If you want a guarantee,
That's wishful thinking.
However if you want to improve your love life,
There are definite things you can do.
Scrutinize before you bind.
Don't leap! Take your time.
If a love you want to keep,
Always have love in your heart.
Never waver, stay on the path you start.

MY THOUGHTS NO. 21

One day your love will come.
With a lot of merriment and some.
Beautiful words, enchantment talk.
Plenty of joyful things for both to do.
Ah! The sky so radiant above.
Flying by a beautiful dove.
Your mind consumes a passionate spirit.
And all the attention you give it.

MY THOUGHTS NO. 22

HATE

God is love, the Good Book says.
How can you love and hate?
Hate can destroy the hater.
It seldom worries the hated.
So why bother?
You can be happier,
Focusing on those you love.
Share the plan of the God above,
Love, love, and love.
Prune your heart and make a new start.
Eliminate hate.
When you do,
You'll feel better too.

MY THOUGHTS NO. 23

To be caught up in passion and love
At first sight is so romantic.
It shows how love can capture the day,
Even though the committed words you do
not say.
The moment is too precious to go into that,
It has to be later for that chat.
All and all you are bound this day,
You're at your zenith, that's all in play.
Nothing will interfere or get in your way,
No cares now what tomorrow will say.

MY THOUGHTS NO. 24

To risk your heart on one
You aren't sure of
Is sheer folly.
It's a map for heart destruction,
As well as the head.
If stability is what you seek,
It's a lifestyle your love must meet.
Try honesty, commitment, and a will,
To stay in a love that's true.
A love and passion with only you.
Plod alone for the one you choose,
Then your chances are good.
Getting a love that's honest and true.

2011

MY THOUGHTS NO. 25

To take the blows and get up
And strike back is commendable.
It shows the resolve to take the heat,
But not a defeat.
Often strength rises during a crisis.
Life doesn't end with a broken heart,
You fix it and make a new start.
Follow your mind and take your time.
A committed love will certainly show,
Scrutinize and apply the wisdom you know.

2011

MY THOUGHTS NO. 26

When the fire dies,
It's too late to scrutinize.
Then come the lies,
A love turned upside down.
The flowers are overwhelmed by weeds,
What a dramatic change to a love in bloom.
Whatever was heavenly is dashed into hell.
However there is a door that can always be open.
With painful choices to leave or stay.
You must make a stand, it's in your hands.
Mingle with others who care and feel the way you do.
Plunge into a direction that's new.
Be bold, take charge, And if you do,
Your world will change and so will you.

2011

MY THOUGHTS NO. 27

Choices, some are good and some could be better.
Some are romantic, some are painful.
We are inundated with choices.
We are happy when they succeed.
But when they don't, we sigh, maybe cry.
Then how can one defeat the missteps?
Scrutinize before you give romance a try.
Make sure the one you care,
Have the same views you share.
Don't fall short.
Take your time and be smart.
Jump with your head then drag your heart.
For sure a wonderful affair will start.

2011

MY THOUGHTS NO. 28

I saw a lovely playhouse,
High up in the tree,
Filled with childish pleasantries.
Mimicking the adult world,
With innocent play,
Escaping hours on a routine day.
Fairy tale are written with this in mind,
To captivate and keep you aroused,
All the time.
Why isn't this world joyful such as this?
Like that enchanting tree house,
Fill with endless bliss.

2011

MY THOUGHTS NO. 29

There is a time for us to take our place,
Among those who traveled to that site,
All of us must embrace.
Sleep greets us, but life goes on.
We who remain should look at the love,
And happiness shared during those joyful days.
Love never dies,
It remains in the heart and mind
Of those left behind.
There is a moment for grief.
But when it cease,
We return to our normal ways.
We'll always remember and carry in our heart,
Unlimited love that will never part.

2011

MY THOUGHTS NO. 30

Quest for the Perfect

Perhaps if you reach that celestial land,
You will certainly find that perfect man.
But is perfection something you are looking for?
Maybe you are seeking a good man.
They are out there, not easy to find.
Yes, you can.
Take care and mingle,
With those who share your goals.
Spend your time,
With loving folks, living the lifestyle you care.
Love yourself and what you do,
The chance is good, you'll find a love that's true.

2011

MY THOUGHTS NO. 31

To My Friend

When you cling to doubt, what can you begin,
When you feel you can't win?
To accomplish your goal,
You must have faith in your role.
Doubt springs defeat.
Confidence is a winning hand.
Life is not easy.
Pain and suffering is everywhere.
You can gripe.
You can cry.
But it won't go away
Unless you take a stand,
And change your plan.

Love you and what you do.
To feel better, you must love you.
To do better, you must make the right moves.
With love in your heart, plan your goals.
Believe you can,
Achieve whatever is at hand.
Pick your friends, the ones that's true,
And share your values too.
Put love in your life.
And when you do,
Others will love you too.

2011

LOVE CHOICES

They laughed and joked about many things.
They even thought of having a fling.
Time went by as they profess their love.
Later they joined the college club.
The same college they attend.
Took similar classes they could blend.

The crowed hollered as they made their way,
With degree, showed it with fun and play.
Marriage was just around the way.
They answered the preacher, had their say.

A happy family with three kids now,
A reserved soldier was called to war.
Family and friends hugged, kissed, and cried,
They gave their hero final goodbye.
Off to the war the soldier went,
To serve his country, a proud gent.

Tears and cries were heard everywhere.
Missing in action, the soldiers said.
Years later he was declared dead.

A sweet romance bloomed in the workplace.
The widow and coworker fell in love.
An engagement was spread around.
Family and friends were happy again.

It was a beautiful, sunny day,
The soldiers, neatly dressed, came by.
Said, "We found your spouse, he's still alive."
The kids gave a loud cry,
"We have our dad, he did not die."

The wounded soldier came to town.
A paraplegic for a hospital stay,
Hoping to see his family that day.

The wife frozen, a dilemma for sure.
How should she handle two men that's dear?
A critical choice surrounded with fear.

2011

THE LOVE YOU NEED

Does he love you or not?
Love does not need prompting.
It's spontaneous.
It comes from the heart.
Oh! If love was guaranteed
When you commit,
Your worries would be free
From doubt and cheat.
That special one would provide
The love you seek.
Life is not so.
Time surely tells.
Often it's late,
When you need to change your mate.
Prayer is left for you to heed,
And hope another will provide
The love you need.

2011

YOU

I constantly reach out for you,
My heart is filled with pride.
There is nothing I wouldn't do,
To have you in my world
By my side.

I don't know how I stand,
I don't even know if I can.
Put happiness in your life,
And be your loving man.

My dreams are full of hope,
I never change my thoughts.
I start the day with prayer
At my place,
Hoping you'll be there.

I can't get pass,
The sparkle in your eyes,
And the feeling
You'll be my prize.
Oh! My God above,
Look at my life
And bring you love,
Within my sight.
I know,
There must be a way
To have you
In my arms every day.

2012

A GOOD DAY

I woke up this morning wondering
How the day would go.
Thought the movies was a place to escape,
A good drama was all I need to know.
The evening was never too late.

With popcorn in hand and soda too,
Striding with the one I love to date.
Cheerful because I was with her,
Knowing she was my only mate.

The movie was playing while we snuggle up.
We continuously paused and planted a kiss.
In between watching was very tough,
Could not be better than this.

Even though the picture did not make our day,
Our passion blossomed in every way.

2010

A SOURCE OF ENVY

They hugged and kissed,
As though they would never quit.
Two beautiful souls,
Seemed to care.
Captivated in their world,
I observed the smiling faces that readily appear.

Their faces glowed, a joy to see.
The feeling of envy rushed through me.
I imagined I was in his place,
Devoured by the love showed on her face.

But oh! Dreams always end,
You wake up and reality begins.
I know I haven't found her yet,
But I'm sure she's for me to get.

2012

LAPSE OF RELATIONSHIP

It was not unusual to share our thoughts,
And exchange words of interest.
We were two buddies, giving each other a lift.
We told stories, joked, laughed,
And listen to issues that crossed our minds.
Mornings, we would have coffee.
Afterward we went our separate ways.
We were the best of friends.
At least that was my thoughts.
It was an arrangement of equals.
Our path crossed daily except on weekends.
We cared for each other to a certain degree.
How much, I didn't realize until there was a
pause,
Rather an absence.
In other words, she didn't show.

At that time, I did not know why.
It was later when I obtain
Some possible answers.
I asked myself, "What's wrong with me?"

"I did not have these feelings before, why now?"
Looking back, I realized we were partners
Without saying so.

Does she miss me?
I really don't know.
I do know I am at a loss
And crushed.
Love comes, ready or not.
Although I didn't realize it,
Love was in my midst.
I let it pass by.
Now she is not at my side.

Never lose hope,
I have heard that line many times.
For sure I haven't given up.
I have endless dreams,
Wishing fate is not like it seems.

2012

WANTING YOU

That wonderful smile, warmth,
And joy you bring with your presence.
I try to figure how to capture,
The aura you send my way.

I ask myself, "What does it all mean?"
Is it a message to consider?
Or just a friendly way to say,
Have a nice day?
Even though it might be wishful thinking,
I look for more.

The mind can handle a little.
The heart even less.
My wonderful dreams put her here.
But when I awake, she is not near.

I say to myself, "What is this all about?"
There must be greater meaning to life and love.
Something beyond our simple view,
Of passion and feelings.

Even when we think we have it all,
And conquest appears in our sight,
Just one misstep changes our plight.

Oh! Love!
I'm yearning to hold you tight,
Hoping change doesn't rear its might.

2012

A FRAGILE ROMANCE

High school sweethearts were just a beginning.
Their love went further.
In college they enjoyed swimming,
For fun and competition.
Life was bursting with meaning.
By the water,
They shared thoughts and future planning.

After their college days,
Their love blossomed in many ways.
Jobs were available for both to choose,
They claimed the ones that matched their views.

The knot was enthusiastically tied.
They were thrust into an arrangement,
Unprepared and unwise.
Life was not the dream they had.
There were many ups and downs,
Sometimes bad.

They traveled many routes,
That never would end.
They would double back and try again.
Finally they shook hands,
And wiped away a tear.
One said, "May the Lord help us,
Goodbye, my dear."

2012

A LOVE THAT LAST

To love a little or not at all,
That's your call.
But look what you miss,
If chances you fail to take.
Love that will shatter
You like an earthquake.
Love that is precious
And romantic too.
All of these could make
A good life for you.
For sure romance is risky.
There is no certainty,
That love will outlast you.
But if you scrutinize and take care,
Your chances are better that love will bind.
Last and last, till the end of your time.

CRYING

It's not harmful to cry.
Crying can calm the heart
And clear the mind.
It provides an opportunity
To think things through.
Also to meditate and move forward.
The hope is a clearer mind will ensue.
A resolution will evolve.
Your world can change.
And you can too.

There is something about my love,
I don't know just what.
But when she is near,
My heart spins like a Ferris wheel.

There is something about my love,
That brings songs to my ear.
Ah! The way she walks.
The way she talks.
And the way she calls me dear.

Sweet melodies pound in my brain,
I am completely overwhelmed by her charm.
Life has made a complete change,
I am thrust in her caring arms.

There is something about my love
That makes me feel
Like I'm in heaven above.
Oh, I pinch myself,
Is this real?

2010

THE END

When the end comes and sweet enduring
memories cascade endlessly,
The world becomes dark and dreary.
Love and hate often move parallel,
Bound by broken commitments
And shattered hopes.
Betrayed or the betrayer,
Who can I say?
Who can withstand the scrutiny of the truth?
However it is certain unless drastic solutions
prevail,
A change must come and it will.
Love does not end with a failed union,
It picks up and move on

1st Row: Ryan Coogler, Zinzi Coogler,
Zetra Evans, Maria Evans
2nd Row: Zishan Evans, Susana Logrono

Maria Evans, Zishan Evans, Catherine
Evans, Zena Evans, Zinzi Evans

COMPLETE

PIANO/VOCAL EDITION

VOCAL SELECTIONS

with a review and introduction
THE BIRD INTERNATIONAL
presents

ZETTA

A 3-ACT PLAY WITH MUSIC
BY ZISHAN EVANS

BEAUTIFUL SONGS
*

INCLUDING
- WITHOUT YOUR LOVE
- LOVE IS WHAT I LOOK FOR
- TO SEE YOU AGAIN
- IT GREAT TO BE HIGH CLASS
_*AND MANY OTHER GREAT SONGS*

COMPLETE ORIGINAL MUSIC

PORTRAYAL OF THE ISSUE
THAT IS THE MOST CRUCIAL,
CONTENTIOUS AND ACRIMONIOUS
OF OUR TIME

ZISHAN EVANS

CELEBRATED AUTHOR

Happy Valentine's Day!

ABOUT THE AUTHOR

Zishan Evans is the product of a Mississippi and Arkansas family. He was born and reared on Chicago's great south side and in his early youth was a strong adherent of the Seventh Day Adventist Church. Since he was seventeen years of age, he has studied music, creative writing, drama, and the theater. He's attending Chicago's grammar and high schools and earned his college degree in Chicago. He currently lives and works in Northern California.

CPSIA information can be obtained
at www.ICGtesting.com
Printed in the USA
LVHW072158040221
678436LV00030B/1821